A Slip of the Tongue

Also by Belinda Broughton and published by Ginninderra Press

Sparrow: Poems of a Refugee

Belinda Broughton

A Slip of the Tongue

Acknowledgements

Thanks to all who encourage me:

My family, especially Ervin Janek, Hana Edwards,
Miklós (in memoriam) and Sally Janek

Jessie Landsberg (again, thanks so much for your generous guidance back in the days when I was hardly formed)

Hills Poets and Friendly Street Poets,
who published some of these poems

Members of First Draft who worked with me

Poets from these groups: Jill Gower, Graham Rowlands,
Louise Nicholas, Rob Walker, and so many others

And you, the reader

Thank you all.

To Ervin and Hana

A Slip of the Tongue
ISBN 978 1 76041 571 6

Cover: Hana Edwards

First published 2018 by
GINNINDERRA PRESS
PO Box 3461 Port Adelaide 5015 Australia
www.ginninderrapress.com.au

Contents

1

The Shoe-care Kit

Even in shoes, we had a game
of stamping on each other's feet
holding on. I can't remember
when it began; I was a child.

We did it when I was pubescent,
when I was a teenager, when I was an adult.
The last time, I was twenty-nine,
we were barefoot and he was dying.

The next time I saw him
I helped Mum nurse him
for three weeks. Then he died,
we buried him and I came home.

I have the shoe-care kit
with which he taught me
to polish my shoes.
So I polish my shoes.

News for Biddy

It was fun when it flooded and all those people were stuck beside the river. One of them had a tiny baby and no milk, so a plane came and dropped some stuff and Dad butchered a bullock for them.

When that snake reared at me I just ran. I didn't remember I was supposed to stand still, but later I could run faster.

Mum went white when the mail truck came and the letter for my brother was from the government. She turned it over and over in her hands.

That dingo poison didn't kill the old tomcat. One night he came home and slept on my bed but he only stayed two days.

When my dog bit the cane toad, he went crazy, frothing at the mouth and running wild. Like rabies Dad said. Mum's doctor said he wouldn't survive but he went bush and came back after three days.

That poddy foal grew up but he was never strong. He got a tooth abscess and died.

I don't mind that my brother told me Wonky had been sent to market. It's OK to know that even though I'm sad.

When I let that rosella go (the one that knocked himself out on the side of the house) he didn't look back. He flew away very fast.

I didn't let those two pigs go on purpose. They weren't my friends. James was my friend and I didn't let him go. We ate him.

When the chickens hatched one of them couldn't get out of the shell. It took me two hours to pick the shell off but it's OK now and the hen accepted it.

The drake has a very long penis. I think the duck likes it but he pinches the skin of her neck too hard.

One morning when the rooster mated a chook I chucked a rock at him, then I felt funny but chooks don't like it I reckon.

That blind chook is getting fat because I put her in the grain bin every morning.

Most of the eggs from that nest in the hay were rotten. We ate the ones that didn't float.

I got glasses for my eyes. They are round and they make me look pretty. I can see all the leaves on the trees.

I got really embarrassed when I pissed my pants because that boy made me laugh too hard.

When I go to boarding school there will be lots of kids to play with.

To Butcher a Bullock

To butcher a bullock you need a bullock.
You need sharp knives and a sharpening stone, and a couple of big men (because they are heavy, you know.)
Best to let them do the bullet bit. Actually best to let them do all of it, really. I do, but then I am only eight.
When it is dead, you can come out from behind your tree and watch the blood flow down the little trench in the dirt.
Amazing, the skin mostly just slips off, and then you can spread it out under the beast while you open it and let the gut spill out.
It's amazing what is in there. The colours: yellow fat, blue veins, white gut covers, and red of course, meat, and blood.
The kidneys, the liver and the heart, almost purple.
And all this interesting stuff has a function. I mean think about it. It all has a function.
What's this for? What's this for?
My big men heap the intestines to the side after they get the good bits out.
Then they cut up the carcass, whole legs and sides. They put it on plastic in the back of the truck.
But I loose interest. I poke sticks in holes and sing to fairies.
We bring the meat home. It's already dark. They hang it on the clothesline to let it set.
Before the flies get up in the morning, they haul it into the meat room and cut it into cuts. Piles of meat. They bag it. Label it. Mince it. Freeze it.
Then when it is all safely stowed away, one of the men goes out with the tractor to bury the carcass. I don't go. The flies know about it and the heat starts the gut swelling and smelling.
But he will bring home the skin and hang it over the fence.
You never know when you'll need some greenhide.

The generator is on. It will need to be on all day.
My mother melts down the fat and pours it into tins. We had brains and liver for breakfast because they are best the first day.
All the bulls are in the house paddock. They come and rut around the clothesline. They screw up their noses and bellow. They can't smell the difference between this blood and a cow's heat.
The dogs are happy. They carry their big bones like trophies.

spinifex

spinifex
dot painting
country

In Droughts Like That

In droughts like that
crows gloss black and gloat.
Carrion eaters are welcome, needed
when air is rank and days are spent
roping dead cattle/roos,
and dragging them
from waterholes.

In droughts like that
water can kill a beast,
the last straw after walking so far
from the last straw of grass
white skeletons also
like eating paper.

In droughts like that
men's eyes bleach pale.
Sunshine comes even from the ground
and the sky is empty and never quite blue
for days and years.

In droughts like that
men's shoulders lower.
Their hats seem wider
over brows that furrow
and crack like dried mud.

On the Sheep's Back

I thought graziers were called squatters
because of the way they'd squat in the dust
to spin a yarn or draw a map.

I didn't realise it was because
they were squatting on the land
or that possession is nine-tenths of the law.

I remember them squatting together
and breaking silence like bread
to speak of seasons and pasture:

those men in their hats sitting comfortably
on the sheep's back, in silence mostly.
They learnt the silence from their fathers

who learnt it from their fathers
who brought the sheep out here
and cleared the land of trees

and people
and then kept silent
until their son's and their son's sons

had never heard speak of it
while their sheep grazed on the grasses
and the grasses grew on the blood

of people who's footprints had marked
the land for seasons beyond counting.
Before sheep.

And I never heard speak of it
nor read of it in the black text
of those green hardback schoolbooks.

About Dad

My father studied clouds
but for months at a time
there were none.

At sundown he hung up his hat
and took off his boots.
He washed his face and hands.

Mum moved the hose and chopped the vegetables.
I fed the chooks and closed the gate
behind the last stupid bum.

Night rose from the east,
easing its purple cloth over the sky, in increments.
Later I lay on the lawn with my father.

He studied stars too – not their meanings or placement,
rather that they were there at all
like so many glittering grains of dust.

Rain came eventually
and the grass grew taller than men.
The cattle were sent to market and the bills paid.

All the children grew up, left home
and there were no more worries.
Perhaps that's why

he didn't wait long after that to die.
He'd finished his studies.
He'd paid his dues.

Mum's Sandalwood Fan

1

The men yell 'Yah! Yah!' The gates clank
and the weaners bawl in the cattle yards.

The stockmen burn sandalwood to heat the brands
incense of charred flesh, dung and men's sweat.

The huddling calves low as buzzing motorbikes
drive their mothers away. Quietness settles with the dust.

2

The scent, the delicate scrollwork would have reminded her
of tea in fine bone china and ladies in some book or other

and who gave the fan to her and which Christmas
and whose fine hands crafted it somewhere far away.

I never saw her use it. She only ever
fanned herself with a newspaper.

The Blown Kiss

Mother, this really is the last visit.
This is the last time I will
hold your hand of knuckles
and kiss your soft crepe skin.

We speak of nothings:
the weather, politics, the body,
other superficial topics, even though
there are things I would like to know,
missing pieces from the puzzle of my life:

why I have this sadness,
the history of certain objects,
who's who in the album of ancestors.
I would like to ask
about: recipes, timelines, connections,
who I am, who you are.

I would like to blame you for some things
and absolve you from all responsibility.
I would like to say, 'Thank you.'
I would like to say,
'Thank you, God bless and good night'

but I don't say, 'Thank you'
and I don't say, 'God bless.'
I just say, 'Good night'
and blow you a kiss from the door
and you blow me a kiss

and when I glance back
you are patting around the bed
for the newspaper, your glasses, a pen,
something lost.

I don't yet realise that the blown kiss
is one of the gestures we share,
one of the little bits of you
that I carry, unchanged, into the world.

I will teach it to my granddaughter.

wildflowers

window gazing
with my clothes half packed
the ringing phone
                    inevitable news
                    each needle on the pine tree
                    is completely still
silence
the phone receiver
in my hand
                    packing
                    Mum's laughing photo
                    dawn
airport clatter
getting the tickets
my hands shake
                    my sister's face
                    at the bag carousel
                    the jostling crowd
in our greeting
our emotions restrained
bags in the boot
                    flying foxes
                    black in the dusk sky
                    stories of her
dark of the moon
all the lights in the house
on
                    feeding
                    the resident magpie
                    body-viewing day

her soft skin
serene against satin
my shallow breath

wildflowers
adorn her coffin
voices waver

soul
spelled S – O – L – E
our amused eyes

rose petals
fall from our hands
veiled earth

on my shoulder
my brother's hand
glaring sunshine

between us
tears and laughter
scotch and ice

her hand mirror
eyes that look like hers
are looking back

Kingdom Come

We asked the priest, who was intent
on sprinkling her coffin with holy water,
to tone it down. We were very Low Church
when we were into it. We learned 'Our Father'
in our beds and were asleep before 'Amen'
He was good, Father John; he let us run the show.

So we wore pink and showered her coffin with petals.
We sang 'All things bright and beautiful' and quoted Leunig.
We told some funny stories, but mostly stories of love.
Father John talked of Kingdom Come,
but we reckon she'll be happy enough with earth.
Soil and God were one and the same, to her.

Empty Room

All done, all packed and folded up,
the knick-knacks distributed.

Only her glasses are on the bench.

salt

of tears
of amniotic fluid

still connected

after all

this

time

A ring, a ring of roses

A ring, a ring of roses is circling the vase,
centred on the table, reminding me of her.
When my mum had babies an old friend said,
'Always do your flowers, Dear. They outshine the mess.'

So she always did her flowers in the morning, in the dew,
a ring, a ring of roses, a posy in her hand,
a tissue, a tissue for the pricked-finger blood,
and very soon the petals, they all fall down,

and very soon the rest of us, we all fall down.

Having a Bit of Mum in Me

My mother is taking over my face.
It began with my body
my attitude, my stance.

Photographs betray her:
head thrown back in laughter,
or standing by a tree
watching her youngest
scoop tadpoles from a puddle.
I know it isn't me
because I'm in the puddle.

'Got a bit of Mum in you'
said my brother last time.
I really can't ignore it now
with one eye on the mirror
and the other on the clock.

List of Kisses

Goodnight kisses from Mum and Dad
Enthusiastic kisses from my siblings
        designed to suck out my brain
Coming kisses, going kisses
Kisses of dogs
The first adolescent kiss
        with that boy at the back of the theatre
        among the kilts and the peasant shirts,
        the smell of stage make-up,
        the heave of the belly
Supermarket kisses, full moon kisses, headland kisses
Kisses on the fluffed head of my infant daughter,
        the smell of her
Her learning-to-kiss pressure kisses
The last kiss from Dad when he was so sick
        that he couldn't close his mouth
The last kiss from Mum, Happy Christmas, she said
        It was August
Hello kisses, goodbye kisses
The kiss of the sun
Kisses with my Love each night before we roll over:
        Goodnight sleep well. You too my Love

My Paternal Grandmother

How the old ones dissolve into the earth,
fade from memory, become history.
The woman who bore my father,
whoever she was,
is in some grave somewhere,
far from where she was born
far from the ones she loved,
wild oats slapping against a headstone.
I have a photo of her: already an old woman
leaning on a stick.

Perhaps my daughter's children
will know her from this photo
but will they care?
Why should they care?
They will love the ones they love,
grow and grieve and
disappear into the earth.
Memories of us reverberate
for a little while and then are gone.
And that's OK, but I would like
to know who she was,
my paternal grandmother.
I would like to know if I
would recognise myself in her eyes.

To Lot's Wife

What did you expect to see,
looking back

the loves of your life, the green river banks,
your fragile babies, the strong arms of your sons?

It was over and you knew it. All that was left
was bones, burnt buildings, cursed soil.

All that was left was salt: you either become it
or you cry it. Either way it dries you up in the end.

Not looking back would have been worse,
the years of grief, the arthritic joints, the slow desiccation.

Be thankful, one glance
was enough. And then it was over.

2

birth

the birth canal
is hard and narrow
but I am a soft egg
I am expelled
wet and flailing

air rasps my skin
and my throat
and inside me
I wail it out
but it comes
rushing back

it is my own voice
that shocks me most

I sleep
as still
as water
and wake
alone

the dull air
is full of sound
that is not
her
heartbeat

Jim

Jim was a diver: a master of falling
– downward twists and spins,
then a slender parting of the water.
A gymnast, he was also a master
of landing the right way up.
It served him well for falling off things.

He taught me breaststroke.
'Swim like a frog,' he said.
'Make your arms move like this
and,' he said, 'do the same with your legs.'
It was so simple and the water
parted as my hair parted,
poured off my face
even as I was taking breath.

He showed me his dick when he was twelve.
'Oh yuck,' I said, and he just laughed.
He'd painted it when he was three,
green, with house paint, oil-based.
His mother told me that. It's a secret.

My Brother's Magazines

When I was ten
I found my brother's magazines
with the naked women
squeezing their breasts together.

I put them back quickly
but did a little drawing
of a woman in lace
with bare breasts.

Then I tore it up
into very small pieces
and ran off
down the back behind the tank

where my hands found
a wet and secret place of me
shocked and delighted
by the shivers.

Then I went to the feed shed
and sat in the cool grain
with my bare legs
and my mind turned

to more important matters
like feeding the chooks.

That Night

And what a sight: that old wooden church
gutting itself into the tinder of that night
and us in our nighties with our bare legs.
The old wooden dormitory clicked
its joints all night in the heat
and two hundred girls slept
with frowns amongst their pimples.

I was twelve and I was homesick
and I was afraid and then I got
my period for the first time,
the brown blood greasing in my knickers,
and that just confirmed how much
I wanted my mother.

Schoolyard Brawl

I've got my face squashed against her breasts,
my arms tight around her. I can feel her
muscles rippling as her fists pound my back.
Luckily she is more brawn than resolve
so she doesn't think to grab my head.

The two girls who put her up to it look disappointed.
Their eager smiles have gone. This odd love dance
is not what they expected at all. They wanted blood
and they would have got it if I hadn't ducked
between Marie's punches and grabbed her like this.

She is calming down. I say, 'I don't know
what they told you but they must have lied.'
She stops punching me and I step away
from her full breasts. What she should do is punch
the shit out of them, but they are her friends, apparently.

Church

The priest's voice drones on
about something other
than the bumps on his head
that look like horns.

Two hundred girls with polished shoes,
two hundred hymn books, two hundred voices
and louder than the whole school,
the old woman at the back, off key.

Paint cracked and grey on the lofted ceiling
and on a ledge behind the priest
above the cross, two pigeons love-cooing,
arching their necks and bobbing,

while the priest's voice drones on
about something other.

The Dormitory

Shirley was a big muscly girl
who slept in the dormitory
between the window and me.
Once she told me,
'If you hold your body all tense
and tight for a while, it will
let go and your body
will shudder and shake
and feel wonderful.'
She said she sometimes
did that at night and if
I saw her shaking
that's what it was.
'You should try it,' she said.
So I did try it but nothing happened.
It was easier to masturbate.

The Last of My Virginity

I got rid of my virginity
when it lost me a man I really liked.
I had been breathless for Alex
for at least a year but he was leaving.

There was a party and I ended up
in his bed, naked and excited
but still refusing to have sex. He said,
'I didn't think you were that sort of girl.'

Being 'that sort of girl' had cost me
a lot of time with Alex so I had a cry,
went on the pill and offered my virginity
to the next attractive taker.

He had red hair and pink sheets
and candles that made our skin look so lovely.
He nodded when I said I was a virgin
but he didn't believe me.

When I bled he was so shocked
that he stopped screwing me and sat
on the end of the bed holding his head.
'Losing your virginity should be special,' he said

but I didn't care. I just wanted
to be done with it and done with it I was
but Red Hair refused to have anything
more to do with it.

Alex hitchhiked home to Perth apparently.
I was told he had to protect his bum
from one particular truckie.
I'm not surprised; he did have a nice bum.

At Twenty

Gone
the moon
and the fairies
I cast off
I leave
the comfort of the summer home
with its rainbows and milk
I leave
the child's hopeful imaginings
I leave
the safe sure deep sleeping past
I leave
the swelling wounds
from crosses
and martyrs.

I lie
smoking
and drinking filth
I sleep by the light of day
I awaken
to neon lights
and tatters of lives
and unsure sexual liberations
men of all kinds
turn and look as I dance
I blindfold myself
and I tell lies
dreadful untruths
to my watchful
inner
I.

To Gregory Black

If you hadn't spat on me
when we were twelve
I wouldn't hate you to this day.

And if it hadn't been
hawked-up green golly
I would have known what to do.

But as it was I just stood there
as it dribbled down my uniform
wondering if I had a tissue in my pocket.

I wanted my Saturdays off
instead of copying out the dictionary
so I didn't punch you in the face.

You laughed too loudly. I reckon
you embarrassed yourself. I reckon
when I meet you in the street,

you remember. Does it hurt?

Flying

I began flying before I grew wings.
In those days I could just swim
in the air or zoom about as if
I had jets on my feet.
That was after I left school
and began growing into myself.

Flying is a very good way
to escape pursuers, men
you aren't interested in,
or embarrassing situations –
anything dangerous or awkward
and I'd take to the air.

Then one day, a very nasty man
was chasing me, so I took off.
It was such a relief to be able
to get away like that.
Trouble was, he started flying after me
and that was that; I never flew again –

even though, eventually, I grew these wings.

Open Until Six

Outside the department store
the young couple
are juicing in their knickers.
She is sitting on a ledge with her
white-socked calves wrapped around him.
He is standing in her four-limbed embrace
and my guess is he can't move aside
for the erection he's sporting.
I try not to stare so I stare
at the grey-haired woman
below me on the escalators.
She is staring at the couple,
the pale face of the girl over his shoulder.
It is Valentine's Day.
The loud speakers urge us
to express our love with gifts.
They are open until six.

Coorong Man

Across this expanse of lake,
salt hardened and crisp,
you expect to see
emus with their long legged stride
and other animals whose tracks you've seen,
kangaroos, wombats –
honeyeaters and pigeons,
because you hear them in the bushes.
And crows fly over the white lake
calling their stark cries.

What you don't expect to see
is a naked man, tall and loose,
his long limbs walking easily over the lake,
his penis bouncing with his stride.
A dog tags him and you could imagine
they are walking on water
if you weren't standing
on the hard surface of the lake yourself.
He doesn't look aside
and you busy yourself
with your easel.
What would you do
if you caught each other's eye?
Wave?

Armpits

Yesterday I shaved my legs
the long hair piling up with the soap
against the razor. I only do it
in summer. Likewise my underarms
if I am going to wear a sleeveless shirt.
The other day I was camping with friends.
It got surprisingly hot so I put on a sleeveless shirt.
Nobody took any notice of my armpit hair
except Joshua who had a long look.
I mean he's not a young man, hasn't
he seen armpit hair before? It amused me
but in his look was a whole array
of suppositions. I don't mind
being mentally undressed by him
because he's beautiful and I love him,
but it was odd, an old friend like that.

Orchids

Talking about sex was something
you didn't do. That's why my old aunt
could not abide orchids with their
overt sex all crinkled and fleshy,
their come-hither tongues, their
silken throats oozing with nectar
and open, their scent like seduction.

On my veranda just now
Dendrobium Kingianum hangs out
her many pink tongues, the nectar
of her desire flirting with spring breezes.
Her flowers are so tiny even my aunt
could look into them for a moment
or maybe not; it's only a matter of scale.

firetail finch

the finch bobs a silly dance of desire
a long, fine twig a-beak

she is impressed
and in their tiny flurry of sex
the twig falls
as a feather
lightly

The Weeping and the Wailing

after Catullus *Poem 3*

Granted it was a very sweet thing – the little finch
she loved so much – hopping around like a wind-up toy
and twittering in her ear. And it would settle in her lap
as if it really loved her. Certainly it trusted her.

It's dead. That's sad don't you think? I mean
it's always sad when something so sparkling with life
lies in your hand as still as a corpse, because it is a corpse,
a delicate thing on its one-way trip to nothingness.

But the weeping and wailing and gnashing of teeth,
she's cried more tears than the size of the bird,
out of all proportion. But then, who am I to say,
hard-hearted bastard that I am; all I care about

is how red and swollen her beautiful eyes are.
There, there, Darling, cry your tears on my shoulder;
let them out; be done with it.
Now, come to bed.

Fig Leaves

Adam's belly was tight with seriousness and blind faith.
He knew nothing of sensual delights or even animal instinct.
He was on his rock waiting for God I think.
He was lean with fasting. Meanwhile I was retching
on my desire and curiosity, growing thin
on stars and water. I wanted words and ideas,
vivid opinions, something more interesting
than the garden. Then I met the serpent.
He understood my predicament and boredom.
He shared with me some secrets he'd learnt
when he was in God's good books –
that there is so much more and we can know it.
'Well,' I thought, 'I've had enough of basking
on lawns all day. Give me some stimulation.'
So I enticed Adam down from his rock
and we shared a bit of knowledge.
I'd been so used to him hanging around on rocks
that I hadn't even noticed his superb body.
The sex we had was so intense it was embarrassing,
hence the fig leaves, besides which later
we could strip them off each other.
God heard our moans. That's what woke him up.
He didn't have a lot to say because he was so jealous
but he cast us out of his paradise into the rest of his creation.
Out here there is this minor problem of death
but the sex is still good.

3

The Belly of the Pot

When I fell for him
it was in the pub
the first night we met.
There was a pot there,
a small red glazed urn
and he talked in his
curious accent about the
belly of the pot and
traced the back of his
index finger over it
as if it was a real belly
or a breast. That was it.
Of course I ended up
in his bed and after
some years was bearing
a belly like that pot:
his daughter. And now
she is bearing a belly
like that pot and I'm
still angry that he got
sick at all, let alone
died, even though he
was a shit. I would
have liked her father
to watch her swelling.

Poem to My Daughter

This is to my daughter Hana
who looks nothing like me
but carries my mother's hands
and my father's nose.
How I tried to protect you
but life dealt out its lessons
and you counted your tricks
and learned things I couldn't
have taught you, things it takes
hard knocks to learn.
Firm, that's what you are,
strong, kind, resilient and brave,
standing there at the death bed
of your father, another thing
I could not save you from,
standing there, looking like him,
carrying his face.

Between Us

He was earth to her – the ground, the soil, the fertile land.
And it was true that seeds sprouted in his hands,
vibrating their blind cotyledon leaves towards the light.
To me he was like the sea – the sea on stormy days,
its deep calm centre barely visible
below the fidgeting glossing quicksilver waves.
But he must have been earth
because it got him in the end.

After he died I went with her to his house,
the house he'd built from scrap.
It was filled with art and with him:
the polish of the step from his feet,
the tilt of the lamp above his chair.
I felt like a ghost – as if I was looking
from a long way off at his tangible world –
his bed, his sheets, his pillow.

A small object was in the middle of the floor.
We don't know how it got there.
It was a gourd I gave him when we were lovers.
I had painted it with fertility symbols:
a red triangle, a little hen and lots of dots.
I stood in his bedroom next to our daughter
and turned it over in my hand and I felt as if
we had spoken of what was important
in the end.

Morning Sickness

Our fearless daughter's belly is swelling.
She is being drawn, spluttering,

into a whirlpool of probability
and chance.

It is unusual for her to lose control –
the strong one, the wilful one.

Her sure feet swell.
Sweat beads on her brow.

The ground below her
is heaving towards the moon.

Our fearless daughter will learn to ride
the ancient waters of her own blood.

Evening

Elephants before sleep
croon their last deep rumble of sound
and reach out to touch each other.

It's evening and we
are winding down towards sleep.
My daughter and her husband
sit on the couch.
She is a fertile mound of belly,
as round as a world.
He drapes his hand across it
listening with touch
to the nudges and squirms
of the one inside.

Soon it will erupt from her
to breathe air and make voice.
Meanwhile we wonder
who this well-known stranger is.

day one

I catch him
between engaged tones
yes! yes!
all over my note pad
the baby's name

the new father
holding his first newborn
looks up
and, before our greetings
humanity

her pale skin
and bandy-legged walk
I greet
this new woman
who is my daughter

my grandchild
sleeping and waking through
her first day
her tannin eyes
the deepest pools

the old man
holds the swaddled newborn
with his calloused hands
they gaze at each other
as if comparing notes

Birth Day

The newborn baby gazed at us,
unblinking.

That first day her eyes focussed
and holding them
was to be in a primal space,
ancient and vast.

Her father gazed back, stunned
by his life's central initiation,
by the birthing of his child,
by the power of raw life.

His wife waddled back from the loo,
pale and puffy and in some pain.
She said, 'Hello, my little one,'
and kissed the soft sweet head.

Her stepfather and I exchanged glances.
We saw our daughter in that moment,
the one we'd nurtured,
that funny little thing,

and she was woman.

First Meeting

Your newborn eyes look and look –
deep gazing. They are space before time.
They are the night sky more ancient than stars.
The sponge of your mind is making connections:
your mother's face, your father's face,
their boundless love surging with blood.

You will make your self,
your ego, your hardened mind,
all the requisites of living as a human.
And in old age, naturally, you will unmake them again
until your eyes brim pale and vast,
with the deep peace of timelessness.

In between is joy and pain,
this amazing world of ten thousand things,
the world you will love,
the world you are discovering
with your newborn eyes.

The Sleep of Mothers

The young mother sleeps
like a wet rag
beside the bassinet
where her baby
skitters through dreams,
bobbing on the surface of them
like the plastic duck
on her bathwater,
tap-tapping
the edge of the tub.

The mother sleeps until
the first faint whimper
wakes her enough to reach
over the edge of the bassinet
and place her hand
on the child.

This is how she snatches
another few moments of sleep,
her arm hung
out there in the cold,
her eyes tight,
desperately
dozing.

Things I Didn't Tell Her

I birthed a daughter and she, a daughter.
We croon around the crib.
The infant twitches and dreams
with her eyes open.

My daughter mothers like I mothered,
with delight and awe,
with her heart open and bleeding.

There are things I didn't tell her:
a familial disease that may result
from pregnancy, details about birth-giving
and the pain of mothering,
that she will ache, her eye focused
on the child, that she will always ache.

Oh, my daughter, this human pain
that connects you to all mothers,
that connects you to all children
and to the people into which they grow.
This is the only pain
I willingly pass on to you.

My job is done.
I will hang around awhile,
will love you both
with the heart of a mother
and the careful detachment
of a grandmother
and then I'll go home.

4

waiting

and the sun
sets
and it rises again
each time
more
surprising

Palm Reading

I probably shouldn't admit that
reading his palm made me move
in with him. That would seem
superstitious and I'm really not
superstitious. Neither do I know
anything about palm reading.

He had said, 'Why don't
you and your daughter move
in with me and my sons.'
And I'd said, 'Why?' and
he'd said, 'Because you
are unhappy.' And I'd cried.

So we were making small talk to
lighten the situation and I picked up
his hands. Blunt hands, soft and
slightly plump, large square palms
with delicate fingers. 'Like mine,'
I thought. And the lifeline and
the one above, set apart, like mine.

It wasn't noticing these things,
but holding his hand like that,
it was as if I recognised it, as if
my body knew his body.
I'm not talking about lust,
just this knowing, like looking back,
like memory.

The Cold Made Us Dream

In the winter, the cold made us dream.
Far from light and sundew melons,
far from sunflowers and the nests of birds –
we dreamed of meat – warm and quivering,
too fresh for the knife. We dreamed
of points of light completely covering
the night sky. Stars we called them.
We were sure frost came from them –
that frost is sparks of light that fall to earth
all through the long night – freezing.

Also we dreamed that if we held each other
a little skin of warmth would build between us
and glue us permanently together. Therefore
we made love often and called it marriage.
Later we learned how to dream birds and their nests,
all manner of vegetables and fruit, and eventually
we dreamed the whole world of flowers
all streaming with nectar and oozing colour into
bright sunlit mornings. That is how we created
mornings. That is how we made spring.

evening, Katarapko

there is no breath of a breeze
the cloud and the river are lit
with the light of stars
and the western glow
of early night

a mopoke echoes its own hollow song

a quiet remorse of loneliness
rings around us
we, who stand together
looking at the pale river at our feet

shall we walk on it? he asks

the bed we made

after hair-prickle
palpitations
our vermilion hearts

stroke skin
sweet as days spent
breathing each other
intimate as earlobes
safe as doonas

later, dreams runkle sheets
twitch and tangle you
feather you away

wake my love   wake
nasturtium-sweet with pepper   us
safe   together   us

under quilt I made
under roof you made

Poppy Field Dream

I would like to hold you as a lifesaver would
above the dark surface of your dreams.

I would like to enter your sunlit field,
and for the poppies to not turn to blood.

I would show you how the petals
attach so delicately to the calyx.

We would celebrate the yellow styles
dusting pollen onto bees' heads.

Oh yes, come with me.
You can protect me and I you

and the poppies will remain poppies.
Let's make a bed of petals

and lie down there, make love and sleep,
the sun warm, the sun warm.

a slip of the tongue

he's into zen bosom, he said
the mother of the moment –
zen bosom – suckling him
and that snail of Issa's
is still climbing Fuji
and somewhere someone
is chopping wood, carrying water

Coming Storm

The storm announces its presence
with thunder, approaches steadily from the west.
It is early night.

Nothing could be more peaceful than my soft bed
and sleeping man with his sweet breath, or this
our golden age – kids grown, good health, not yet old.

Still, the storm rumbles towards us,
flashing its blue light and scaring the dogs.
One whines softly; the other shakes beneath the bed.

I lie against my man and watch
the world flicker and quicken with gusts.
He puts his arm over me.

Waking and Sleeping

He says he likes to watch me
in the morning when he wakes –
my face all wrinkled and serious.
He says he's never seen a more serious sleeper
and that is why he is always tempted
to stick his finger in my ear –
that and my immediate indignation.

For my part I like to listen to him roll to sleep
after the flagellant crescendo of his orgasm
when all the stresses and energies of the day diffuse
and his breathing slows and deepens
and after a few twitches, grunts, perhaps a fart,
he gives a few snores, so I give him a shove
and he wakes enough to roll over, saying,
'I was snoring. I heard myself. I woke myself up.'

juice

these days your hair
is white enough
to see in moonlight

we've grown old together
like socks
a little worn and holey

even so we fold up nicely
tuck together knee to knee
bum to lap and our bodies

are as warm and soft
and misshapen
as flannelette pyjamas

the wind is strong tonight
one of the trees fell
I hope we are safe

and that I'll wake
in the morning to you
bringing me orange juice

Mantova couple

Archaeologists in Italy (near Mantova) have discovered a couple who were buried 5,000 to 6,000 years ago, hugging each other.

hold still my love   the dawn breaks
as I always said   it would
for 5,000 years   at least
I have held   your bones
beautiful   even
in death my love

hold still my love   the earth
that has been our blanket
and our cocoon   parts
the sky   (so long unseen)
is   as sky was
when we had eyes   to see it

oh my love   they dismember me
bone   by bone
remember me   and the long night
of our secret   embrace

Forty Years

In 1963 I was bandaging the old dog's belly
with strips of cotton torn from a bed sheet.
The dog stood patiently with her head lowered.
Later she stepped from the rags lightly, as if dancing.

In 1973 some girls at the boarding school
hissed at me. Others laughed openly.
I sought out small dark spaces
to lick my wounds.

In 1983 a bubble in my belly grew into a baby.
It was born from me, kicking and twitching in the sharp air.
It was such a surprise to be an animal,
lactating and with my fangs bared.

In 1993 the child looked like a sprite,
was falling down and getting up, bandaids on her knees.
Play fights involved teeth and claws, barbs and spit bombs.
I couldn't save her from the world at all.

In 2003 the house was quiet and empty.
My husband and I fretted in our sleep,
woke, padded the floorboards with bare feet.
We wore our old scars like badges.

A Little Drawing

There is a drawing I did of my father.
It falls out of unexpected books at unexpected times.
The paper is yellowing like the memory.
It is his death mask and so serene.

He had a high forehead and a long nose
and was tall enough to look aloof
if it wasn't for the fact that his heart
shone from his eyes, at least for me.

In the drawing his calm face lies amongst flowers
his strong nose, his relaxed eye,
his peaceful mouth – almost a smile.
What a relief death was, after all that pain.

The flowers are colourful like the church that day.
So many people, so many flowers.
And the shopkeepers closed their doors
and stood on the pavement as we passed,

him in front in the black car.
Strange, I don't remember the graveyard,
only that the coffin went down and down
as if there was no bottom.

And that the dust tumbled from the little trowel,
red, into that dark hole.
I never went back but I did a little drawing.
It falls at odd times from odd books.

After Rain

near Berri

A little rain and this river country
is teeming with insects:
tiny ferment flies and massive gum moths
ants and wasps and grasshoppers
– so many grasshoppers that they
swarm across the land, eating everything.
Everything is eating everything
or being eaten or both.
Nothing new in that, but the scale of it
here in the dry lands after rain!

Fish roil the surface of the water
growing fat on the abundance.
Water-skimmers are so plentiful
that they interlock fine oily feet,
their mandibles all full of something.
Swallows play, zipping and swooping.
Wagtails are so full they can hardly wag
and kookaburras don't need to hunt;
food flies into their beaks!
A tiny bug-eyed fish, barely visible,
brings down a wasp as big as itself
and dragonflies zip above the water
catching small prey in their net of legs.

Strangely, there are no mosquitoes
as the sun goes down on all this eating
and being eaten. Night seeps in,
drawing its soft blanket over us.
The stars prickle the sky
like an elaborate sprinkling of salt.
Everything is still, restful, calm.
And yet, they tell me,
even stars are eating stars.

Trophy Cupboard

I collect my dead like trophies.
I store my mother over here near my father,
my friend Rod in a different place
with a mutual friend who shouldn't be
in this cupboard because she is not yet dead.
I don't know where I put Grannie, but
the various dogs and cats and poddy calves
all have their own dusty corners.
It's odd that, although I don't dust,
those ones from my childhood are getting clearer.

The recent ones are gaudy like cheap brass.
They glitter and catch your eye.
You can still read the dates and the details.
There is my ex-partner, father of my child.
He positively gleams.

There are a lot more spaces in this cupboard
and I am afraid of them.

Between Stars and Trees

Tonight the stars have assembled on one plane
about two miles up.
Science can't convince me otherwise,
not tonight.
Tonight the trees have a tall black presence
and the space between the stars and them
is distinct and full of something –
more than air.
Perhaps it's our loved ones (living and dead)
or our love like beauty
or maybe when the heart is full like this
overflowing with the beauty of it,
maybe the feeling expands above the trees
ringing.
I'm sure if you put your head up there
you'd hear it – music: flute or cello.
In any case the trees are shaking their ears
and even though my warm blood
urges me inside, I won't go yet.
I'll lie here while these sacred trees
quietly shudder
turning the stars off and on
with their shaking.

Not Knowing

In a hammock under a wide sky,
the sun has warmed my slow blood.
The trees above nod when I move.
A dandelion arrives, drifts,
ambles on the delicate breath of air
– this way, that, exits sky left.

I don't know anything meaningful.
I know its Latin name, its method
of seed dispersal, what it looks like
under a microscope.
I know about osmosis, photosynthesis,
xylem, phloem, probability.

But I don't know anything really,
not in this moment of the world,
cradled in the warmth of spring sunshine,
the dandelion afloat on its way somewhere,
the sky painted very high up with long filaments
of cloud and a breeze getting up in the branches.

I'm given over, up,
and I don't know
what I don't know.

My Ultrasound Heart

My beautiful heart.
Really, it is a beautiful heart.
In the static of the ultrasound
beating – dark spaces, light.
The cardiologist explains what's what.
There are four chambers, valves, arteries
and it is pulsating in the common rhythm
filling, emptying – pushing and pulling
my blood to and from my toes.
Its vibrating valves look like thread.
Truly I have a beautiful heart –
so mundane and unremarkable.
No bigger than my fist
doing its thing inside my chest –

it used to be counting up.
These days it's counting down.

Imprint

I slip my foot into your print.
It's like wearing your shoe.

My father's shoes are empty.
Spiders build webs and time passes.

Sometimes he comes to my dreams
and we say, 'But you're dead.'
and he says, 'Shh.'

I wake.
I get up.
I stand in my own footprints
and I walk.

Lightning Source UK Ltd.
Milton Keynes UK
UKHW02f1013280818
327916UK00009B/412/P

9 781760 415716